COVER TO COVER BIBLE STUDY GROUP

Acts 1-12

CHURCH ON THE MOVE

CWR

Christine Platt

Copyright © CWR 2010

Published 2010 by CWR, Waverley Abbey House, Waverley Lane, Farnham, Surrey GU9 8EP, UK. Registered Charity No. 294387. Registered Limited Company No. 1990308. Reprinted 2014.

The right of Christine Platt to be identified as the author of this work has been asserted by her in accordance with the Copyright, Designs and Patents Act 1988, sections 77 and 78.

See back of book for list of National Distributors.

Unless otherwise indicated, all Scripture references are from the Holy Bible: New International Version (NIV), copyright © 1973, 1978, 1984 by the International Bible Society.

Concept development, editing, design and production by CWR
Cover image:istock/Jean Assell
Printed in the UK by Linney Group

ISBN: 978-1-85345-574-2

Contents

Introduction

Prepare to be challenged and amazed!

The book of Acts is set in a red-hot rebellious geographical area during a tumultuous time in history. The Roman Empire had stamped its iron boot over much of Europe, North Africa, Egypt and the Middle East, including Israel – the Jewish homeland. Nowhere was there more intense hatred for the Roman invaders than in Israel. Josephus reports that during the first century there were 10,000 incidents of insurrection in Israel.[1]

Against this backdrop Jesus had come and preached His message of freedom, hope, restored relationship with God and fulfilment of the ancient promises to Israel and the whole world. Jesus' message, healings, miracles, life, death and resurrection had been carefully documented by Luke, a physician and close friend of the apostles. Of the Gospel writers he is the only one to have written a sequel detailing the growth and expansion of the Early Church. So it is through his careful penmanship that we have this precious document starting with Jesus' last words to His bewildered followers. The account continues with the spectacular gift of the Holy Spirit who then propelled these same followers into courageous exploits to birth the Church in Jerusalem.

Jesus, however, had more expansive plans than just a local ministry to Jewish people in Jerusalem, and these now Spirit-empowered believers were thrust into wider ministry to the Gentile world. We are deeply indebted to Luke for making available to us this amazing story. Some have given this book the title of The Acts of the Apostles, but others have felt this is too man-centred. A more apt title might be The Acts of the Holy Spirit.

'Acts shows the church in its finest hour – under fierce

attack but unstoppable, spiritually aflame, morally pure, impelled by love, and bound together by the living presence of Christ. It details a movement of pioneers and risk-takers breaking new ground, taking on new challenges, highly energized for assault on spiritual ignorance and wickedness.'[2]

In the Gospels Jesus was limited to His physical body. Acts shows Him in action through many other bodies and speaking other languages, but it is still His story. He is the star of the show. Jesus continues to be the star of the show as He works in and through us – His people – in our world today.

Luke is the uncontested author of this book and he wrote it in AD 63, soon after the last events recorded occurred. Some scholars think it was written slightly later in AD 70. However, we can be confident that in Acts we have a detailed account of an eye-witness at this momentous time in history.

Speeches form about 25 per cent of the narrative of Acts. Ajith Fernando in his commentary on Acts points out that: 'They [the speeches] are most certainly summaries and paraphrases of much longer talks, and they faithfully report what was said.'[3]

He identifies the main themes in Acts as follows:
• The priority of evangelism
• The power of the Holy Spirit
• Community life – with special concern for the poor, as in Luke's Gospel account
• Teaching
• Prayer
• Breaking human barriers in Christ
• The place of suffering
• The sovereignty of God
• The Jewish reaction to the gospel
• The legal status of Christianity.[4]

Chapters 1–12 cover the period from the gathering of the frightened, confused group in Jerusalem after Jesus' crucifixion to the beginnings of the Gentile Church – a huge culture shock for Jewish people. The rest of Acts covers the development of the Gentile Church and expansion to Europe – Rome.

As many of us today have the stimulating privilege of living in multi-cultural societies among people of many and varied beliefs, there is much we can learn from the believers in Acts. Luke doesn't gloss over mistakes or problems. He tells it like it is – failures, successes, joys and sorrows are all recorded.

When we seek to move out of our 'Jerusalem' and take the message of Jesus to 'regions beyond', we too will encounter failures, successes, joys and sorrows. But this need not discourage us. We walk in the footsteps of pioneers who have paved the way. Let us be faithful and courageous as we continue to write the story of Acts, empowered by the same Spirit as the early believers.

My prayer is that as you study these chapters you will be inspired to take greater risks in loving, giving and sharing Jesus with friends, family and strangers. The sky is the limit! We are empowered by an indefatigable Spirit who longs to pour out His gifts for ministry and to produce His fruit in our lives.

Notes

1. Flavius Josephus, *The Wars of the Jews*, 7 vols. Of *The Works of Flavius Josephus*, translated by William Whiston (Grand Rapids, MI: Associated Publishers and Authors n.d.).
2. *The Book of Acts: The Smart Guide to the Bible* series, Robert C. Girard, series ed. Larry Richards (Thomas Nelson, 2007. GRQ Inc.) p.3.
3. Ajith Fernando, *The NIV Application Commentary: Acts* (Grand Rapids: Zondervan, 1998) p.29.
4. Ibid. p.30.

WEEK 1

The Wind Beneath Our Wings

Opening Icebreaker

Think about when you've had to wait for something, like starting a new job or having a baby, and you weren't exactly sure what would happen. How did you feel?

Bible Readings

- Acts 1 and 2
- Ephesians 1:15–22
- John 14:15–27

Opening Our Eyes

Forty amazing days

Theophilus, a Roman official of high position, was the chosen recipient of this sequel to Luke's Gospel. We are now privileged to peep over his shoulder and read it for ourselves. Having finished his Gospel with some of Jesus' post-resurrection appearances and His ascension, Luke now gives more details of those forty amazing days between Jesus' crucifixion and His ascension to God's right hand (see Eph. 1:20–21). In His conversations with His followers Jesus seems to have concentrated on two main topics: the kingdom and the coming gift of the Holy Spirit.

'Your kingdom come, your will be done on earth as it is in heaven' (Matt. 6:10). In God's kingdom everything is focused on doing His will. The entire universe is under His sovereign control. Whereas to our human minds there are many incomprehensible things happening in our world, because He is the Lord Almighty, there are no random events – there is a throne in heaven and a King sits upon it who reigns supreme (Rev. 4:2–3).

Despite having spent three intensive years with His disciples, Jesus still found it necessary to reassure, teach and correct their false assumptions. They had in mind an earthly kingdom for Israel free from Roman tyranny (Acts 1:6–7). Jesus had already promised them the Holy Spirit of truth, who would continue to teach them the way to go (John 14:15–27). Now He promised them the Spirit of power who would enable them to spread His message throughout the world. He would be the 'wind beneath their wings'. After these momentous days Jesus ascended to heaven in accordance with His own prophecy (John 14:28–29). In the midst of the disciples' confusion, fear and excitement they decided to do three things:

- Concentrate on prayer together (Acts 1:12–14) – women are specifically mentioned, characteristic of Luke.

- Be obedient and wait for the promised gift
- Recruit another apostle (1:15–26).

Wind, fire and language!

Ten days of earnest prayer and growing expectancy brought them to Pentecost – the Jewish barley harvest festival (fifty days after Passover). Jerusalem was bursting with pilgrims. Suddenly people heard a great whoosh of sound, but there was no wind, and saw fire, but nothing was burning up. (Wind symbolises the breath of God and fire the presence of God.) There was utter astonishment, but what really stopped people in their tracks was to hear uneducated Galilean men talking about God in fifteen different languages so that all could understand!

Acts 2 is a perfect demonstration of the subjective (feeling) and objective (knowledge of truth) necessary parts of Christian experience. Some revivals have floundered because insufficient attention was given to the need for clear exposition of biblical truth. Some churches focus their energies on theology to the detriment of the Spirit's empowering presence. In Peter's carefully reasoned sermon he made sure everyone fully understood what God's prophecies meant and what God now expected of them. These God-fearing Jews realised they had killed their long-awaited Messiah. No wonder they were 'cut to the heart' (2:37)!

The priorities of the new community were:
- learning doctrine from the apostles
- fellowship – encouraging one another in their faith
- breaking of bread – shared meals
- prayer.

Chapter 2:42–47 is a precious window into the world of the Early Church. The ongoing result of the Holy Spirit's empowering was joy, miracles, boldness and fruitfulness in witness, unity, sharing, care for the poor and worship.

Discussion Starters

1. **a.** What scriptures would you show to someone who doubted that Jesus has risen from the dead?

   _____

   _____

   _____

   _____

   b. What other biblical evidence might you offer to a doubter in Christ's resurrection?

   _____

   _____

   _____

   _____

2. What was Jesus' strategy for reaching the world with His love and truth (1:8)?

   _____

   _____

   _____

   _____

3. Why is it unwise to try to predict Jesus' second coming (1 Thess. 5:1–11)?

   _____

   _____

   _____

   _____

4. What qualifications were required for the apostle to replace Judas?

   _____

   _____

   _____

   _____

5. **a.** What happened when the Holy Spirit was first given?

_____

_____

_____

_____

b. What was the significance of these signs?

_____

_____

_____

_____

c. What was the response of the crowd?

_____

_____

_____

_____

6. Why did Peter refer to the Old Testament in his sermon?

_____

_____

_____

_____

7. How do people receive the gift of the Holy Spirit?

_____

_____

_____

_____

8. What impact did the gift of the Holy Spirit have on the community of early believers?

_____

_____

_____

_____

Personal Application

The gift of the Holy Spirit transformed all those who received Him. Some changes were dramatic and immediate, others more gradual. The fruit of the Spirit is a lifetime work of development (Gal. 5:22–24). His gifts are usually given in embryo form and need to be 'fanned into flame' (2 Tim. 1:6) by study and practice.

What changes have you already noticed in your life? What other change would you like to see? Add this to your daily prayer. The Holy Spirit will work powerfully in your heart and mind. He will prompt you how to co-operate with Him as you seek to 'live by the Spirit' and 'keep in step with the Spirit' (Gal. 5:25).

Seeing Jesus in the Scriptures

Jesus made sure that His apostles and followers were as prepared as possible for their task of taking to the world His message of truth and freedom from Satan's power. He was patient with them to the end of His earthly visit. After humbling Himself to become one of us, He now sits at God's right hand, 'far above all rule and authority, power and dominion … God … appointed him to be head over everything for the church, which is his body, the fulness of him who fills everything in every way' (Eph. 1:21–22).

Praise Him for the privilege of being part of His body for the short time of your earthly existence. Keep in mind this picture of Him being 'far above all rule and authority, power and dominion'!

WEEK 2

God's at Work!

Opening Icebreaker

What opportunities have you had recently to share the gospel?

Bible Readings:

- Acts 3:1–26; 4:1–31
- Psalm 119:9–11
- Hebrews 10:24–25

Opening Our Eyes

Why so surprised?

Beggars were a common sight at the Temple entrance as devout Jews were expected to give alms. No doubt Peter and John had given money many times. What made this day different? We can only assume that God's Spirit prompted Peter and John to especially notice the crippled man … and a mighty miracle of healing took place. May we too be sensitive to the Holy Spirit's prompting as we go about our normal daily activities.

It is instructive to note that Peter and John went about as a team, which is the normal way of working in the New Testament. Jesus sent out His disciples two by two (Mark 6:7; Luke 10:1). When Peter went to visit Cornelius he took six brothers (Acts 10:23b; 11:12). Paul rarely travelled on his own. There is safety, strength and encouragement in not being alone.

The cripple's response was understandably exuberant. This miracle could not be hidden in a corner. Light had clashed with darkness and everyone witnessed it. Peter took advantage of the situation to preach – not focusing on the miracle or himself or John but on the One who made it all happen. This is in marked contrast to the disciples squabbling among themselves about who was the greatest (Luke 9:46; 22:24). Peter had learned well his lesson of humility.

Peter used some intriguing names for Jesus during his speech: God's servant who suffered – (reminding his hearers of Isaiah 52:13–53:12), the Holy and Righteous One, the author of life, the Christ, a prophet like Moses, leaving the people in no doubt that they had killed their promised Saviour. He then focused on the necessity of their personal response to Jesus – 'Repent … and turn to God'.

First official resistance to evangelism

The religious leaders were seriously upset. Not only were Peter and John talking about Jesus whom the Sanhedrin had condemned as a blasphemer, they also claimed He had risen from the dead (the Sadducees didn't believe in the resurrection of the dead), and to cap it all Peter and John were not officially sanctioned teachers! How dare they teach! In their anger they made the grave error of having the apostles arrested and put in jail. This only increased the interest of the ordinary people and the Church grew. Peter, the ever eager preacher, got another opportunity. The Holy Spirit filled him with boldness, wisdom, passion and brought relevant scriptures to his mind. The leaders were dumbfounded. They could only repeat their threats and let them go.

Response of believers

On their release Peter and John's natural response was to go quickly to tell their friends what had happened. Fellowship was vital to them. The believers' prayer is a pattern for all of us facing crises:

- They prayed together.
- They praised God – 'Sovereign Lord' – nothing can thwart His plans, the enemy has limited power.
- Their prayer is full of Scripture – drawn out of a deep knowledge of God's Word (Psa. 119:11).
- They took a long look at God and a brief glance at their problems.
- They didn't ask for protection or for the problem to go away, but for ability to be obedient and for God, by signs and wonders, to confirm that He was with them.

God's response

God knew His traumatised people needed reassurance, so hefty angels were dispatched to shake the building – not too little, not too much! This experience emboldened them all in their witness.

Discussion Starters

1. What changes would the beggar need to make in his life now he was healed?

2. What response do we need to make when we experience God at work in our lives – eg an answer to prayer?

3. How can you grow in becoming more aware of the Holy Spirit's prompting in your daily life? (Gal. 5:25)

4. What was the content of Peter's gospel presentation?

5. What can you learn from Peter's gospel presentation that you can apply in your own life?

6. **a.** What is the principle that Peter and John articulate in Acts 4:19–20?

_____

_____

_____

_____

b. How does this relate to respecting our leaders and government? (1 Pet. 2:13–17)

_____

_____

_____

_____

7. What enabled Peter and John to be so eloquent and bold?

_____

_____

_____

_____

8. Review the 'Response of believers' section of Opening Our Eyes. How can you grow in 'taking a long look at God and a brief glance at your problems'?

_____

_____

_____

_____

Personal Application

Wouldn't we all love to be effective evangelists? We are thrilled when we hear stories of how others have led people to the Saviour. Along with the thrill we are perhaps saddened to find a tiny bit of jealousy and disappointment at our own lack of fruit. Maybe you've prayed for years without seeing your loved ones bow the knee. What do you do?

I have not yet discovered any magic bullet, except to not give up. Acts encourages us to seek the Holy Spirit's empowering, to be courageous and skilful in sharing the message, and to spend time with Jesus, allowing Him to mould our character to be more like Him. Then our lives will carry the fragrance of Christ, which will attract seekers (2 Cor. 2:14–16).

Seeing Jesus in the Scriptures

Scripture is unequivocal in its insistence on the uniqueness and supremacy of Jesus. 'There is no other name under heaven given to men by which we must be saved'. We need to beware of being seduced by the present culture of religious pluralism – 'All roads lead to God, don't they?'

As the Good Shepherd, Jesus goes out to seek the lost, who then need to come for salvation through Him as the one and only 'gate' (John 10:7). Our deeply compassionate Saviour sees His confused, bewildered creation stumbling along blind alleys. He not only leads His followers along to intercept the wanderers, He uses all other means – dreams and circumstances – to open windows of light into darkened souls. They then can choose ... but He remains the Only Way.

WEEK 3

'Without bleeding the church fails to bless'

Opening Icebreaker

What stories do you know about persecuted Christians in today's world?

Bible Readings

- Acts 4:32–37; 5:1–42; 6:1–7
- Joshua 7:1–26

Opening Our Eyes

Good sharing

As with most communities, in the Early Church some people were wealthier than others. The unity and love of believers for one another radically changed their attitude towards possessions – it became 'ours' rather than 'mine'. But they didn't all immediately renounce their goods in a gigantic jumble sale. This was not New Testament communism. They exercised wisdom. Often those whom God blesses with wealth have more financial expertise than those of us on lesser incomes, and they need to keep exercising that wisdom for the benefit of all.

Those endowed with greater resources observed the needs of those around them, liquated some stuff and came to a central point for distribution (the apostles), so that no one could be accused of favouritism or partiality. There was integrity, accountability and sacrificial generosity. In this context Barnabas, a key figure in Acts, is introduced to us as a specific example of good sharing. He truly lived his name – Son of Encouragement.

Bad sharing

This is the emerging Church, warts and all. The dishonesty of Ananias and Sapphira at the beginning of the New Testament Church mirrors Achan's greed and dishonesty at the birth of the Old Testament community (Josh. 7:1–26). We see clearly God's determination that His people should be holy.

Peter was not frightened or discouraged by God's swift and dramatic judgment, nor was he concerned about upsetting a large donor. John Stott uses this incident to outline some helpful principles as regards church discipline. He points out that 'It is a good general rule that secret sins should be dealt with secretly, private sins privately and only public sins publicly.'[1]

'Without bleeding the church fails to bless'
– Bishop Festo Kivengere

The apostles were having a ball – miracles, healings, church growth abounded – every day the adrenalin pumped. Satan was seriously displeased and stirred up jealousy among the religious leaders. Putting the apostles in prison was like trying to hold back a tsunami with a cricket bat. Nothing – not imprisonment, flogging or threats would inhibit their boldness – in fact it merely emboldened them. How often do we rejoice because we have been counted worthy of suffering disgrace for the Name?

One can't help being amazed at the closed minds of the religious leaders. Despite daily miracles in the marketplace, powerful expositional preaching by Peter, being puzzled by the miraculous release of the apostles from prison, they would not believe in Jesus. The human mind exercises tremendous power – for good and evil. Let's make sure that our minds are open to the Holy Spirit so that we can carefully evaluate all that we hear and see, and be brave enough to admit when our cherished convictions turn out to be wrong.

Conflict resolution

This cross-cultural clash was satisfactorily healed. It had all the potential of poisonous disunity. Under the guidance of the Spirit, the apostles listened well to this grievance, took decisive action and involved all the believers in the decision-making process. Everyone was communicated with. They delegated wisely, not feeling pressured to sort it all out themselves. They then affirmed the people's decisions by commissioning the men chosen. Crisis averted. Everybody happy. Oh that all conflicts could be resolved so beautifully!

Discussion Starters

1. Why was it important that gifts for the needy were brought to the apostles for distribution and not given directly to individuals?

_____

_____

_____

_____

2. What implications does this have for your gift-giving?

_____

_____

_____

_____

3. What can we learn from this incident with Ananias and Sapphira?

_____

_____

_____

_____

4. What does Bishop Festo Kivengere's statement: 'Without bleeding the church fails to bless' mean in your life?

_____

_____

_____

_____

5. How could you develop more of the apostles' attitude? 'Day after day, in the temple courts and from house to house, they never stopped teaching and proclaiming the good news that Jesus is the Christ.'

_____

_____

_____

_____

6. Why did the Twelve not want to take on the job of food distribution?

_____

_____

_____

_____

7. **a.** What qualities were required for those to be chosen to be responsible for the distribution of food?

_____

_____

_____

b. Why were these qualities necessary?

_____

_____

8. Why was it important that the apostles 'prayed and laid their hands on [the Seven]'?

_____

_____

_____

_____

9. What principles of conflict resolution did the apostles use?

_____

_____

_____

_____

Personal Application

I wonder how many of us, especially in the Western world, would have been convinced and brave enough to join the early believers. The apostles didn't attempt to make the gospel more palatable in order to win converts. The new believers knew they were coming into relationship with a holy God who hates sin.

It's tragic when people are led into the kingdom with false promises of peace and joy without a clear understanding of the need to renounce sin and change their lifestyle. How about you? Are there areas in your life that are not under His lordship? Are you willing to make hard choices to put Him and His kingdom first?

Seeing Jesus in the Scriptures

Jesus had walked with His apostles for three life-changing years. They had seen Him teach, heal, suffer, die and ascend to heaven. He had trained them well, and they, in turn, now empowered by the Holy Spirit, were teaching, healing, suffering and would eventually die and be welcomed into heaven.

Despite disappointments, discouragement and huge opposition Jesus finished the work of teaching and training His apostles before He fulfilled His mission of the redemption of the world. His earthly life was full of purpose and ultimate meaning, and He pursued His calling with single-minded dedication to the glory of His Father. 'I have brought you glory on earth by completing the work you gave me to do' (John 17:4).

Note
1. John Stott, *The Message of Acts*, The Bible Speaks Today (Nottingham: IVP, 1990) p.112.

WEEK 4

Church on the Move!

Opening Icebreaker

Which verses of Scripture have you used to encourage yourself or others when encountering difficulties?

Bible Readings

- Acts 6:8–15; 7:1–60; 8:1–4
- Luke 21:12–18

Opening Our Eyes

First New Testament martyr

Stephen, as one of the chosen Seven, was considered 'full of the Spirit and wisdom' (Acts 6:3). He also did miracles (6:8), even though he was not an apostle. As an overseer in the distribution of food he probably worked among the Synagogue of the Freedmen (6:6–9) – those freed from slavery. While serving in this mercy ministry Stephen also shared the good news of Jesus, which provoked opposition from those who wanted to preserve the status quo. His opponents, however, could not stand up against his wisdom, thus fulfilling Jesus' promise in Luke 21:15.

When serious theological debate failed, the opposition began a campaign of lies, which progressed to a quasi-legal trial and finally resorted to violence in order to rid themselves of this perceived threat. As John Stott says: 'The same order of events has often been repeated … Let others use these weapons against us; may we be delivered from resorting to them ourselves!'[1]

Stephen was accused of speaking against the Temple and the Law of Moses. In his defence he wanted to show his opponents that God was not limited to a specific place, like the Temple, and that anywhere God was, was holy ground. Although the Temple was important and significant, its existence was not a guarantee of God's presence and protection. In this context we would do well to consider what is an appropriate use of church buildings – which part, if any, is holy ground?

Another aspect to consider is that when Jesus found the place of worship and prayer used by the Gentiles taken over and used as a marketplace, he drove out the money-changers and those selling doves (Mark 11:15–17).

In Stephen's speech he covered four major epochs in

Israel's history, where God was actively at work, both outside and inside the promised land:
- Abraham and the patriarchal age: 7:2–8
- Joseph and the Egyptian exile: vv.9–16
- Moses, the Exodus and wilderness wandering: vv.17–43
- David and Solomon and the establishment of the monarchy: vv.44–50.[2]

Stephen's knowledge of Scripture and the Holy Spirit's empowering enabled him to discern truth, whereas the Jewish religious leaders, though steeped in Scripture, were blind to the evidence that God's promised Messiah – the new Temple – had been among them. '[Stephen's] face was like the face of an angel' (6:15), which surely showed that God approved of his words and actions. However, when his opponents could not refute his arguments, their engrained prejudices drove them to commit murder.

Spirit-filled suffering
As Stephen lay dying God vindicated His servant by filling him with His Spirit and giving him a vision of heaven. When faced with gross injustice and furious aggression Stephen remained winsome. As the stones crunched into his flesh, his prayers echoed those of Jesus when on the cross (Luke 23:34,46). The fullness of the Spirit is present for all believers even in the darkest moments.

Satan makes a huge blunder
Misdirected zeal whipped up a ferocious desire in Saul to destroy the Church. Believers were imprisoned, others fled for their lives. But – and it's a glorious 'but' – wherever they went, they preached the gospel! For seven to eight years the Church had been mainly focused in Jerusalem. It was time to spread its wings. The expansion is reminiscent of what happened in 1949 in China. Hundreds of missionaries were expelled, but the national Christians multiplied, even under traumatic persecution. Satan cannot outwit God. Our Almighty Deity will always have the last word.

Discussion Starters

1. How is Stephen described? (See Acts 6:8,10,15.)

_____

_____

_____

_____

2. Why were the members of the Synagogue of the Freedmen so opposed to Stephen?

_____

_____

_____

_____

3. How should we respond when we hear teaching we are not familiar with?

_____

_____

_____

_____

4. In the light of Stephen's speech and Jesus' actions in Mark 11:15–17, what do you consider to be an appropriate use of church buildings?

_____

_____

_____

_____

5. How was Stephen enabled to stand firm when encountering such opposition?

_____

_____

_____

_____

6. In what ways can you increase your knowledge and understanding of Scripture, so that you too can stand firm in difficult times?

_____

_____

_____

_____

7. How can Acts 8:1–4 encourage believers when encountering problems and setbacks? (See also 2 Cor. 5:7.)

_____

_____

_____

_____

8. What other biblical incidents demonstrate this same truth?

_____

_____

_____

_____

Personal Application

Stephen's godly response to injustice and aggression shows he had a well-developed theology of suffering. He knew the risks he was taking in spreading Jesus' message, and was prepared for the consequences.

In today's more hedonistic world some of us get surprised by suffering as though life should always be comfortable and pleasant. Do you skip difficult parts of the Bible and focus solely on the promised blessings? Yet we follow a crucified Saviour who suffered, as have many of His followers.

Prayerfully meditate on Romans 8:18: 'I consider that our present sufferings are not worth comparing with the glory that will be revealed in us.' Ask God to help you come to a biblical understanding of suffering as a believer.

Seeing Jesus in the Scriptures

For devout Jews the Temple in Jerusalem was the focal point of their worship, because God was there. They travelled long distances to enter its courts to pray and bring offerings.

But Jesus said: 'I tell you that one greater than the temple is here' (Matt. 12:6). When He died the curtain dividing the Holy of Holies from the worshippers was ripped apart (Matt. 27:51). No more separation!

As New Testament believers we have the immense privilege of being able to worship Jesus wherever we are – at home, at church, on a moonlit beach, or waiting in the rain at a bus-stop. He is worthy to be praised at all times.

Note
1. John Stott, *The Message of Acts*, The Bible Speaks Today (Nottingham: IVP, 1990) p.127.
2. Ibid. p.130.

WEEK 5

Gospel Explosion!

Opening Icebreaker

In what ways did God prepare you to accept the gospel message?

Bible Readings

- Acts 8:5–40; 9:1–31
- John 4:4–42
- Galatians 3:28

Opening Our Eyes

Philip on a mission

Philip, one of the chosen Seven 'full of the Spirit and wisdom' (6:3), made a stupendous, courageous decision. When persecution erupted in Jerusalem he followed the example of his Master (John 4:4–42) and journeyed to a most unlikely place – Samaria – a region with 1,000 years of mutual hostility between Samaritans and Jews. Not the easiest place to start a new mission! The Samaritans were not considered by Jews as 'true Jews'. They had intermarried with other nations. They only accepted the Pentateuch – the first five books of the Bible – thereby rejecting all the prophetic and wisdom literature of the Old Testament, but they were waiting for a Messiah figure.

Philip launched himself into this hotbed of antagonism and preached Jesus and did miracles. Many believed and were baptised, including Simon, a sorcerer. It later transpires that Simon was seeking power, not a relationship with God.

But something strange was happening and Peter and John heard about it in Jerusalem. Although these new believers had repented and been baptised they did not receive the Holy Spirit until Peter and John came and laid hands on them. This two-stage experience has generated much discussion in the intervening 2,000 years.

John Stott explains that because of Jewish–Samaritan hostility there would have been a danger of there becoming a Jewish Church and a Samaritan Church. Therefore apostolic recognition was vital for this ground-breaking outreach as a public sign of acceptance of Samaritan believers on the same basis that Jewish believers were accepted. In this way the Church would be united. John Stott sums up as follows: 'there is no biblical warrant for a two-stage Christian initiation as the norm, or for the practice of an imposition of hands to inaugurate the supposed second stage.'[1]

Philip was a true pioneer. He not only opened up the Samaritan mission field, but God also gave him the privilege of leading the first African to Christ. The Ethiopian was probably Jewish by birth or conversion and a God-seeker. God saw his heart and sent him a teacher. There were no supernatural signs, but he believed and was baptised. Philip was ready to do mass evangelism (in Samaria) and then leave this highly fruitful ministry in obedience to God and make a long journey to meet up with one lone searching heart. He shows he was also skilled in personal evangelism.

The Damascus Road
Saul's is probably the most dramatic and well-known conversion. Luke considered it highly significant – he includes the incident twice more in Acts (22:3–16; 26:9–18). There was lightning, a voice, the last post-resurrection appearance of Christ, blindness … not many of us can identify. However, there are similarities. All of us need a personal meeting with Jesus. All need to respond humbly in faith and repentance and all will receive a call to service.

Throughout three long, dark days Paul prayed and waited. Another brave man, Ananias, came to him calling him 'Brother Saul'. That must have been like the sweetest music to Saul's ears – the persecutor being warmly welcomed as a brother. Being accepted by the Jerusalem church was another hurdle – Barnabas to the rescue!

It is hard for us to grasp the magnitude of these new ventures and the outstanding courage of Philip, Ananias and Barnabas who, by their obedience, paved the way for Jesus' last words in Acts 1:8 to come to fruition.

Discussion Starters

1. What was the effect of Philip's ministry in Samaria?

2. How did Peter know that Simon's profession of faith was insincere?

3. What should we look for in a genuine profession of faith? (Acts 2:38,42–47.)

4. What qualities did Philip have that equipped him to be a witness for Christ?

5. How could you grow in developing these qualities?

6. Why was Saul so vehement in his persecution of Christians?

_____

_____

_____

_____

7. What was Saul's response to the 'light from heaven'?

_____

_____

_____

_____

8. Why did God use Ananias to bring healing to Paul and not send an angel?

_____

_____

_____

_____

9. In what ways can you encourage new believers and seekers into your fellowship even if they seem the most unlikely people?

_____

_____

_____

_____

Personal Application

In Acts 1:8 Jesus promises power from the Holy Spirit to enable us to be witnesses for Him on our home patch and further afield. Witnesses tell what they have seen and heard. What is your story today? What have you seen and heard that you could share? A vital element is to tell your story in a way your audience can understand, depending on their age, life experience, culture, previous exposure to Christ-followers and/or the Bible. This requires careful Spirit-led thought. Prayerfully choose two or three people you know and compose a few sentences to share your story in a way appropriate to them. Talk about these with a Christian friend. Ask God to give you opportunities to share your story over the next week.

Seeing Jesus in the Scriptures

Jesus' power is vividly demonstrated throughout these passages. He empowered Philip to do miracles and heal people. His power crumbled the bitter antagonism of the Samaritans. He cracked open the fanatically stubborn heart and mind of Paul. He made a way for a searching African to find the truth. He gave Peter discernment. He strengthened Ananias and Barnabas to face difficult and dangerous situations. Nothing is too hard for the God of all mankind (Jer. 32:27).

His power is the same for each of us today. What is even more encouraging is that His 'power shows up best in weak people' (2 Cor. 12:9, TLB).

Thank You, Jesus, that we don't face life on our own, but You promise to be with us and pour Your power into us.

Note
1. John Stott, *The Message of Acts*, The Bible Speaks Today (Nottingham: IVP, 1990) pp.152–158.

WEEK 6

God Writes a New Chapter

Opening Icebreaker

What are some big changes that you've experienced recently and how did you feel about them?

Bible Readings

- Acts 9:32–43; 10:1–48
- Ephesians 2:11–22

Opening Our Eyes

Aeneas, crippled for eight years, was spectacularly and instantly healed. Peter then told him to tidy up his mat. Why? Was Peter concerned about keeping the house neat? One reason might have been that Aeneas needed to remove all reminders of his past sufferings so he could fully embrace all the challenges and changes that healing brought into his life.

This is a healthy principle to live by. As we receive forgiveness and love from God we need, with God's grace and help, to rid ourselves of memories of past hurts or mistakes and not allow them to fester.

Tabitha (Dorcas) had an epitaph to be envied: 'a disciple … who was always doing good and helping the poor' (9:36). Hers was a down-to-earth humble witness. She didn't have an up-front gift of teaching or healing, but she could sew, and she used her gift to the full. In many developed countries governments are trimming welfare budgets. This gives an increased role for the Church to follow Tabitha's example in caring for the poor.

When faced with the finality of death Peter copied what he'd seen Jesus do with Jairus' daughter (Mark 5:35–43). I can imagine that Tabitha sewed with increased passion after that experience! Both miracles resulted in glory to Jesus.

Peter demonstrated a servant heart by making this sudden ten-mile journey to come to the aid of the believers in Joppa. In accepting hospitality from Simon the tanner Peter showed his willingness to reject prejudice and step outside his culture. Those in contact with dead animals were considered unclean by the Jews. Peter is now ready to receive one of the greatest surprises of his life!

Earnest prayer and good works are not enough

By most standards of measurement Cornelius was a good guy, but a vital element was missing. Cornelius had responded to the light he had received. God saw his yearning heart and arranged for the deficit to be filled. In doing so God used Cornelius to mark a cataclysmic change in the Jewish belief system (Eph. 2:11–22).

This required an elaborate plan and timing that could only be God-initiated: an angel came to Cornelius, a threefold vision was given to Peter, a special message came to Peter at a crucial moment, the Holy Spirit came with unmistakable signs.

Just as Peter had been instrumental in opening the door of salvation to the Samaritans, so now he opens the door of salvation to the Gentiles, thus fulfilling Jesus' promise in Matthew 16:19 to give to Peter the keys of the kingdom. Although this was a huge change for Jews, it was not a huge change for God. Right from the beginning His plan had been for salvation to be offered to all peoples (Gen. 12:3b).

'The tragedy was that Israel twisted the doctrine of election into one of favouritism, and became filled with racial pride and hatred, despised Gentiles as "dogs", and developed traditions which kept them apart.'[1] Suddenly Peter realised that his deeply held convictions were nothing but mean, narrow-minded prejudice. In John Stott's words, this chapter is not so much about the conversion of Cornelius, but the conversion of Peter.

The change made Peter and his companions uncomfortable, but they could not deny that God was in it. Change is never easy. May we be as willing to accept God-inspired change as Peter and his companions eventually proved to be.

Discussion Starters

1. What changes would healing bring to Aeneas' life?

_____

_____

_____

_____

2. What helps you to move on from past hurts or mistakes?

_____

_____

_____

_____

3. In what ways can you follow Tabitha's example of caring for the poor?

_____

_____

_____

_____

4. Do you think the dead can be raised today? Why or why not?

_____

_____

_____

_____

5. How did Cornelius respond to the angel and his message?

_____

_____

_____

_____

6. Why did God give the Jews rules about clean and unclean animals (Lev. 11:42–45)?

_____

_____

_____

_____

7. What did the vision reveal to Peter (Acts 10:28b)?

_____

_____

_____

_____

8. Which groups of people are victims of prejudice in our world today?

_____

_____

_____

_____

9. How can we learn to recognise and address our own prejudices?

_____

_____

_____

_____

10. What would help you to break down prejudices in your own community?

_____

_____

_____

_____

Personal Application

Throughout history there have been dark times when God's Church has displayed prejudice and hatred ... but radiant times also when believers have followed their Master's example and reached out in loving acceptance and service to those despised by others.

Followers of Jesus are called to be lights for the world (Matt. 5:14). What can you do this week to push back the darkness that's trying to encroach upon people's liberty and joy? In what ways can you show God's acceptance, love and grace to others, especially to those with whom you don't normally have much in common? Try to see life from their point of view. You might get a surprise just as Peter did!

Seeing Jesus in the Scriptures

If anyone had the right to consider Himself superior to others it was Jesus! He is the Son of the Most High God. In every aspect He is greater than all created beings. But He stooped to become human. From His birth and throughout His life He identified more closely, not with the rich and famous, but with ordinary, unremarkable men and women – like you and me.

'... he set aside the privileges of deity and took on the status of a slave ... he lived a selfless, obedient life and then died a selfless, obedient death ... Because of that obedience ... all created beings in heaven and on earth ... will bow in worship ...' (Phil. 2:7–10, *The Message*). Worship is the only obvious response to such love and sacrifice.

Note
1. John Stott, *The Message of Acts*, The Bible Speaks Today (Nottingham: IVP, 1990) p.185.

WEEK 7

Conflict Resolution

Opening Icebreaker

What are some scriptures that encourage you in your prayer life?

Bible Readings

- Acts 11:1–30; 12:1–25
- Hebrews 11:1–40

Opening Our Eyes

From criticism to praise

Launching a new ministry can give rise to criticism, but such ventures need to be examined by the Church as course corrections might be needed. Peter gives valuable lessons in handling criticism. He knew that entering a Gentile home would offend his Jewish co-labourers, so he took six brothers with him as witnesses – wise forethought.

He listened well to the criticism, then 'explained everything to them precisely as it had happened' (11:4). Criticism flourishes when rumours circulate and people don't fully understand the facts – good communication is one of the keys to settling conflicts. Having heard the full story the apostles and church leaders in Jerusalem had to recognise that this was God-inspired. Once convinced they embraced the change with enthusiasm.

The Jew–Gentile divide is probably not uppermost in our minds, but the principle of non-discrimination is important. In Christ's Body there must be equality of all its members – whatever race, social class or gender they might be.

Pioneers of new ministries are often passionate, eager to get on with the job. It takes time and effort to get support from the wider Body of Christ, but it is time and effort well spent. Another meeting of the Jerusalem Church was necessary to iron out more objections (Acts 15), but they grappled with this issue until agreement was reached. The cosmopolitan city of Antioch was ideal for this first international congregation where Jews and Gentiles worshipped together. The success of this church shows each member's commitment to overlook differences and 'to keep the unity of the Spirit through the bond of peace' (Eph. 4:3). There was potential for massive misunderstandings. No wonder Barnabas decided to recruit Paul as a co-worker!

The prayer conundrum

The church in Jerusalem was in shock. Persecution and suffering were familiar to them, but this was extreme. James had been beheaded. Peter was in prison awaiting execution. No doubt they had prayed for James' safety but God had not delivered him. What to do? The right thing to do and the only weapon at their disposal against the might of Rome was prayer. While the church earnestly prayed Peter blissfully slept – content to trust God with his life or his death, just as Shadrach, Meshach and Abednego had done centuries before him (Dan. 3:16–18).

Peter was spectacularly rescued. He could barely believe it, neither could the praying faithful, but God exercised His sovereign will. Why Peter was rescued and James was not is a mystery, graphically expressed in Hebrews 11.

Herod was frustrated and humiliated. He took vengeance on the guards, then went on holiday to Caesarea. The people of Tyre and Sidon had upset him and needed to mend fences, so an official reception was arranged where they could flatter Herod's deflated ego. Herod, arrayed in pomp and ceremony, accepted the peoples' adoration of him as a god.

In his vast litany of sins this was the ultimate and it was God's time to crush Herod's pride. Although Herod was gorgeously clothed outwardly, inwardly he was rotten with worms and died a miserable, painful death.

The chapter starts with James' murder and Peter in prison. It finishes with Herod's death, Peter free and the gospel spreading. Although God permits tyrants to oppress for a time, He will always have the last word.

This is a significant point in Luke's narrative. The gospel has been preached in Jerusalem, Judea and Samaria … from now on it goes 'to the ends of the earth'.

Discussion Starters

1. What do we learn about Peter's character from the way he handled this criticism?

_____

_____

_____

_____

2. How could you help someone who is the target of criticism from other believers?

_____

_____

_____

_____

3. What do we learn about Barnabas' character from Acts 11:19–26,30?

_____

_____

_____

_____

4. What characterised the church in Antioch?

_____

_____

_____

_____

5. List the miracles that God did in order to release Peter from prison.

_____

_____

_____

_____

6. How did Peter respond to these miracles?

_____

_____

_____

_____

7. What characterised the church which met in Mary's house?

_____

_____

_____

_____

8. In what ways could your church/community/small group/you, as an individual, deepen in prayer?

_____

_____

_____

_____

Personal Application

Maintaining an earnest faith-filled prayer life is a challenge for most of us. Satan will do all he can to discourage us from praying God-sized prayers. In His 'model' prayer in Matthew 6:9–13 Jesus urges us to start with praise: 'Our Father in heaven, we honour your holy name' (TLB). Focusing our minds on God as our Father who loves us and wants the best for us, and who is holy and good, will make even our most outrageous prayers seem quite possible. Faith will rise.

The prayer goes on: 'May your will be done here on earth.' It is His will that we seek. In His sovereignty, holiness and power He knows what is best and our response is to bow our knees before Him.

Seeing Jesus in the Scriptures

The news about Jesus is described as 'good' (Acts 11:20). 'Good' seems such an ordinary word to describe the life-changing, world-changing stupendous gospel!

Through Jesus' death and resurrection God 'has rescued us from the dominion of darkness and brought us into the kingdom of the Son he loves', and in that Son, 'we have redemption, the forgiveness of sins' (Col. 1:13–14). What better news could any human being ever receive in their entire life? Because of their status as accepted, beloved, forgiven children of God Christians should be the most joy-filled people on planet Earth.

Life deals out some tough blows at times but the good news is always relevant. We need to daily live out our identity and thank Jesus for all that the 'good news' means to us.

Leader's Notes

Week 1: The Wind Beneath Our Wings

Aims of the Session
1. To see the impact of the gift of the Holy Spirit in the lives of the apostles and early believers, and to desire that same impact in our own lives.
2. To be empowered to take new steps in reaching out to others with the gospel.

Opening Icebreaker
The aim of this icebreaker is to help people identify with the apostles and followers as they waited. It should help the group to get to know one another a little better, especially if you have a new group.

The Introduction to this study guide gives important background and context to Acts. If your group members haven't read it, give them a few minutes to do that before starting the discussion.

Discussion Starters
1.a. Matt. 28:1–20; Luke 24:1–53; John 20:1–29; John 21:1–25; Acts 1:1–11; Acts 2:24–34; 1 Cor. 15:3–8.

b. The change in the apostles' behaviour from terrified deserters to bold witnesses, risking everything for Jesus – persecution, rejection, imprisonment, martyrdom.

2. Jesus' strategy was to use ordinary people, empowered by the Holy Spirit to witness about all they had seen and heard of Him. They were to start in their home and local area (Jerusalem), and reach into their nation (Judea), cross into those of similar cultures (Samaria) and to the rest of the world (uttermost).

You might like to discuss what this means on a practical basis for your group members – ie what is their Jerusalem, Judea, Samaria and uttermost.

3. The dates of future happenings are known only to God. It is therefore a waste of time and energy and an unhelpful sidetrack to try to predict them. Our responsibility is to be ready for His coming at all times.

4. He needed to be one who had followed Jesus and been with the disciples from the very beginning – John's baptism, through to Jesus' death and resurrection – therefore, a tried and tested witness and co-worker.

5. b. Wind – the breath of God
   Fire – the presence of God
   Tongues – so that everyone could hear the message in their own language. (See also 1 Cor. 12–14.)
   c. The crowd was amazed, bewildered, and had questions; some ridiculed and slandered the apostles.

6. He was speaking to Jewish people and he wanted them to see that Jesus was their promised Messiah that their Scriptures had prophesied about, and not just another prophet or religious leader.

7. From Acts 2:38 – they need to repent, turn away from sin, ask for and receive forgiveness, ask for the Holy Spirit in the name of Jesus, and be baptised – declare their faith in Jesus, usually as a public declaration.

8. See Acts 2:42–47. You could pray over these activities and qualities for yourself and your own community.

Week 2: God's at Work!

Aims of the Session
1. To learn from Peter's gospel presentation and make a practical application about how to enhance the content of our own evangelistic message.
2. To learn from the early believers' response to crises.

Opening Icebreaker
This is not meant to be a guilt trip, but for group members to encourage each other in their own personal evangelism.

Discussion Starters
1. The beggar would now need to try to earn his own living, take responsibility for himself and, out of gratitude, try to help others – be a contributor and not just a receiver.

2. Our response should be exuberant thankfulness and praise to God, and to find ways to encourage and help others.

3. We should be praying daily for the Spirit to prompt us and for a greater receptivity to His promptings. Also, when we become aware that we've missed that prompting, we need to repent and ask for help for the next time.

4. • He focused on Jesus – told them who He was
   • He was upfront with them about their sin and the eventual consequences.
   • He referred to their previous knowledge – ie Old Testament writings.
   • He gave them clear instructions on how to respond to God, and what would happen if they rejected Him.

5. • When people confuse us or sidetrack us with other issues, we need to respectfully bring them back to

the fundamental issue of Christ's lordship and the necessity of relationship with Him.

- We need to be clear about judgment without being self-righteous – stress being saved by grace.
- We need to start with the understanding and knowledge that people already have, so ask questions first to ascertain that. Peter knew that his Jewish hearers would know the Old Testament Scriptures.
- We need to be growing in our knowledge of and confidence in God's Word.
- We need to give clear instructions on how to respond – a relevant booklet can help, such as *What to Say When People Need Help* or *Every Day with Jesus for New Christians,* both by CWR.

6. As far as possible we need to obey our God-given authorities, except when they act in direct contradiction to God's Word. This requires discernment, tact, wisdom and courage. We need counsel from mature godly believers. When our government or local leaders are seriously off track, we need to be respectful and objective in letting them know what we think.

7. The Holy Spirit's refilling, the fact that they had spent much time with Jesus, and their knowledge of Scripture. This might be a good moment to stop and pray these qualities into the group members' lives.

8. Some crises can be utterly overwhelming. This is where we need the support of other believers to help us turn our minds to God and leave the problems with Him. Group members could help each other with this as they share their experiences.

Memorising some God-centred scriptures will also help.

Week 3: 'Without bleeding the church fails to bless'

Aims of the Session
1. To understand the Christian principles relating to evangelism, sharing of resources, being willing to suffer for Jesus and resolving conflicts.
2. To make a practical application in one of these areas.

Opening Icebreaker
This icebreaker is to remind ourselves about the reality that some believers live with. You could have some relevant magazines available if people need a direct reminder. Some organisations involved with the suffering church for example are:
Barnabas Fund (www.barnabasfund.org); Christian Solidarity Worldwide (www.csw.org.uk); Open Doors (www.opendoorsuk.org).

Discussion Starters
1. In this way needs could be met with fairness. If gifts were given directly to individuals without others' knowledge some people might have received abundance and others with possibly less visible needs might not have received anything. The apostles would have had overall knowledge of the needs.

This is a good principle when substantial amounts of money are involved – the donors sold land or houses.

2. Most gifts should be given to the Church and reputable charities, but smaller discretionary gifts can be given to individuals when their needs are known. But care needs to be taken. Some people are highly skilful at making their needs known to many people!

3. Their sin was not in keeping back part of the money, it was their dishonesty – they wanted to appear more generous than they were.

4. This statement implies that suffering is part of the Church's mandate. Some believers do literally bleed when they experience persecution. Unfortunately most believers in the developed world are 'suffering-averse'. We need to develop a more biblical picture of what is involved in following Christ – not seeking suffering, but living a sacrificial life of selflessness.

5. Pray daily for opportunities to share your faith and for the courage to do it (2 Tim. 1:7). Be prepared with a short testimony that is relevant to your listener's understanding. Know the main points of the gospel – you could encourage your group members to follow an evangelism course.

6. They knew their calling was to pray and to share God's Word, and they couldn't get distracted from that. It might be worth saying though that in other instances we need to beware we don't find a reason for not serving in a particular way because it doesn't seem 'important' enough.

7. a. They needed to be known as Spirit-filled and wise.

   b. This was a very sensitive issue and required wise handling. It had the potential of creating a huge division in the Church.

8. To show that theirs was an important task, not an inferior one to the apostles – just different calling. The apostles needed to show that they affirmed the people's decision.

9. • They listened well and took the grievance seriously – they didn't ignore or over-spiritualise the problem.
   • They took decisive action, involved all the believers and communicated well.
   • They exercised leadership – came up with a proposal to delegate.
   • They gave responsibility to the group – did not

impose their own choice of leaders, but gave guidelines about what qualities to look for.
- They commissioned the Seven, accepted and affirmed the people's decision.

Week 4: Church on the Move!

Aims of the Session
1. To encourage deeper faith in God when encountering difficulties and setbacks.
2. To make a practical application to grow in knowledge of Scripture as a basis for deeper faith.

Opening Icebreaker
The aim of this icebreaker is to show that God has given His Word for our encouragement and as a basis for our faith, so we need to use it.

Discussion Starters
2. They thought he was speaking against the Law of Moses and the Temple. They didn't really listen to him, and didn't want to change.

3. We should:
- listen and be willing to change our viewpoint;
- pray for the Holy Spirit's discernment;
- check with Scripture (Acts 17:11);
- ask others' counsel;
- if we disagree, do this in a godly way and not imitate Stephen's opponents by spreading inflammatory lies, but we should stand firm on what we know to be right;
- if we agree, be humble enough to admit we were wrong;
- as far as possible, carefully evaluate the character of the person who is teaching (Matt. 7:15–20).

4. It appears that Jesus' action was prompted by the fact that the Gentiles were being hindered in their worship and prayer because of the bazaar-like activity. Also those selling were motivated more by profit than enabling worship. Stephen's speech indicates that wherever God is, is holy – so the church 'sanctuary' is no more holy than the church café. Therefore all church buildings could be used in ways which advance God's kingdom, which includes serving the community.

5. He was enabled by the fullness of the Holy Spirit and his knowledge of God through Scripture and the teachings of the apostles.

6. There are several ways to take in God's Word:
- Hearing – through sermons, tapes, conferences
- Reading – regular private reading
- Studying – in homegroup, conferences, study manuals
- Memorising – maybe your homegroup could decide to memorise verses regularly
- Meditating – really mulling over verses and passages.

You could help the group make a practical and realistic application to increase their Scripture knowledge.

7. We need to remember that God has a plan even though we cannot see it as yet. He can use setbacks, opposition, even our mistakes for His purposes.

8. You might need to give people some time to think over this question and possibly give them some prompts. Some ideas are:
- Jesus' death – incalculable benefit for all mankind.
- Peter's imprisonment – emboldened the believers – led to prayer and praise.
- Saul persecuting David – those experiences prepared him to be a great king.
- Joseph – his training as a slave and prison inmate

prepared him for his future ministry.
- Moses' parents gave him up. Consequently he received the ideal education for future leadership.
- Hannah's years of being barren prepared her to be Samuel's mother and then to give him up.
- Abraham being willing to go out into the unknown – his faith then became a blessing to the whole world.
- Paul's imprisonments gave him time to write letters, which we have today.

Week 5: Gospel Explosion!

Aim of the Session
To understand more of what it means to be a disciple of Christ in terms of obedience and sensitivity to the Holy Spirit, witness and willingness to suffer.

Opening Icebreaker
The aim of this icebreaker is to show that coming to Christ in repentance and faith is usually a long process of God's gracious promptings and preparation. In this passage the Samaritans had some background knowledge of God, and Jesus Himself had visited there. Paul was steeped in Scripture and he saw Stephen's face looking like an angel and witnessed his godly response to unjust suffering. The Ethiopian had the Scriptures and was seeking to know more.

Discussion Starters
1. Crowds came and listened to Philip's teaching. They believed and were baptised. Evil spirits were cast out. Many paralytics and cripples were healed. There was great joy. Simon the sorcerer also 'believed'.

2. Simon wanted to use worldly means to obtain spiritual blessing. He was fascinated with power, not relationship

with God. When challenged he did not repent. He just wanted to avoid God's judgment (8:24).

3. • Repentance – turning away from sin, change of priorities.
   • Eagerness to hear and read God's Word.
   • Desire to be with other believers.
   • Receive the gift of the Holy Spirit – the *norm* is to receive the Holy Spirit when you believe – not later. The Samaritan experience was special for that instance (see Opening Our Eyes). NB: There will certainly be subsequent 'infillings' of the Holy Spirit. We are called to be continually 'filled with the Holy Spirit' (Eph. 5:18).
   • Care for others.
   • Praise to God.
   • Joy.

4. He was full of the Spirit and wisdom. He had courage and a good knowledge of Scripture (Acts 8:35). He was sensitive and obedient to the Holy Spirit.

5. To develop these qualities we need to ask God for them; also, take time with Him learning to listen to His voice. We also need to work on increasing our knowledge and understanding of Scripture. You could help out on an Alpha course and learn what sort of questions people in your community are asking and how to respond to them.

6. He understood that the old way of Judaism and the new way of Jesus could not co-exist, so one 'way' had to be stamped out. Jung wrote that, 'fanaticism is only found in individuals who are compensating secret doubts.'[1] Paul's experience of seeing the courage, passion and peace of Stephen and other believers may have begun to unravel his convictions.

7. • He recognised it was God – He called the voice 'Lord'.
   • He instantly obeyed.
   • He fasted and prayed for three days – signs of deep repentance and seeking God.
   • He was baptised.
   • He immediately became a bold witness.

8. Paul needed to be connected to the Church. Ananias needed to be sure of Paul's true conversion. Paul needed to be humbly dependent on God's servant. And he also needed the encouragement and acceptance that Ananias brought.

9. Smile, be friendly and inclusive, not judgmental.

Note
1. C.G. Jung, *Contributions to Analytical Psychology* (London: Routledge and Kegan Paul, 1928) p.257.

Week 6: God Writes a New Chapter

Aim of the Session
To grow in understanding and recognising one's own prejudices and take steps to refute them.

Opening Icebreaker
This is to get people thinking about change. Small changes, even getting a new mobile phone, can have elements of excitement but also irritation. Big changes, like jobs, house move, change in family situation, can be an exhausting upheaval (and sometimes involve pain and loss). Change in belief systems usually takes some time to work through and involves the humility to admit you were mistaken.

Discussion Starters

1. Change from a dependent mindset to more independent, ie earn his own living, care for his own needs and those of his family. He would need to focus on the reality of being healed and plan for a healed future, and not live in fear that the paralysis would return.

2. • Forgive others as you have been forgiven (Matt. 6:12). Get help from others if you need it.
   • Take every thought captive to obey Christ and not allow negative thoughts to stay in your mind (2 Cor. 10:5).
   NB: Deep hurts usually take a long time to heal and often require help from others.

3. • Contribute to a food bank.
   • Be alert to needs and try to meet them.
   • Volunteer to use your skills for others – handyman, knit/crochet/sew, cook, computer, accounting.

4. Jesus is the same, yesterday, today and forever (Heb. 13:8). Therefore His power is still available to raise the dead. But both Stephen and James suffered 'untimely' deaths, so we need discernment before praying. Raising the dead was a rare occurrence even in Jesus' ministry.

5. He was fearful, but obeyed immediately. He knew the message was important and showed concern for his friends and family by gathering them. He received Peter with great respect and humility.

6. In the Old Testament every aspect of life was to demonstrate their commitment to God so they were given rules as to how they could maintain ritual purity. In the New Testament commitment to God was to be demonstrated, not by keeping rules, but by living in obedience to the Holy Spirit's guidance.

7. In future he was to make no distinction between 'clean' and 'unclean' people – the barrier between Jew and Gentile was demolished.

8. There are many – here are some:
• Immigrants, especially illegal ones.
• Some people groups: people from Israel, Palestine, Iraq, Afghanistan, Native Americans, Indigenous Australians, Maori, low-caste Indians.
• In some countries, women.
• Disabled – both physically and intellectually.
• Homosexuals.
• The poor.
• The elderly.

9. We need to pray for God to open our eyes. Peter needed a threefold vision before he began to understand. Even mature Christians can have blind-spots. We need to be alert to when we are harbouring any judgmental attitude and repent of it. God's people should be the most accepting, grace-filled community on the planet. Sadly we often fall short, but we need to pick ourselves up, repent, say sorry and start again to try to treat others as God's special beloved handiwork.

10. The basis on which to break down prejudice is to recognise that we are accepted by God by grace alone (Eph. 2:8–9). It has nothing to do with race, intelligence, gifts – it's pure grace. Therefore, none of us is better than anyone else. We need to repent of any superior attitude. We also need to take initiative with humility to reach out to those who suffer prejudice.

Week 7: Conflict Resolution

Aims of the Session
1. To understand some helpful ways to handle criticism.
2. To acknowledge God's sovereign wisdom in how He chooses to answer prayer and to see ways of growing in prayer.

Opening Icebreaker
There will be many, but some examples are:

Luke 18:1–8   Persistence
1 John 5:14–15   God's sovereignty
Phil. 4:6–7   Pray, don't worry
Eph. 3:20–21   He is able
2 Chron. 7:14   Humility
Mark 1:35   Jesus' example

Discussion Starters
1. Peter was patient, didn't get angry or upset. He listened well and gave a full explanation. He understood their concerns because he, too, had struggled to recognise what God was doing. He was empathetic – able to put himself in their shoes and saw both sides of the issue. He honoured Jesus' words by sharing them in defence of his argument. He gave glory to God – simply shared what God, the Holy Spirit had done and left Him to convince them.

2. • Encourage them to listen well and take time to explain their position carefully, clearly and calmly.
   • Encourage them to ask God if any of the criticism was valid, and then repent of any wrongdoing.
   • If there is no resolution, the parties may need to agree to differ … but still aim 'to keep the unity of the Spirit through the bond of peace' (Eph. 4:3).

3. He was respected as a godly man by the church leaders in Jerusalem and entrusted with a special assignment. He was spiritually discerning – 'recognised

the evidence of the grace of God'. He looked for and rejoiced in the positives – no doubt there were problems, but he focused on the good things. He was an encourager – actively sought to build up the new believers. He was good, Spirit-filled and faithful. He was humble – he went to get Saul. He knew Saul had been called as the Apostle to the Gentiles. He willingly jeopardised his own leadership position. He was reliable and honest.

4. • It was multi-cultural.
   • It was growing.
   • It was Christ-centred. The people were called 'Christians'. Even though this may have been a derogatory term, it implies that the believers talked incessantly about Christ.
   • It was responsive to the Spirit – listened to Agabus's prophecy.
   • It was caring and had a broader vision than just their own community – responded to the need of their Jewish brothers in Judea.

5. • He sent an angel.
   • A light shone in the cell.
   • The guards were unable to see or hear anything, yet were just next to Peter.
   • The chains fell off Peter's wrists.
   • All other guards on duty in the prison were unable to see or hear anything, yet were most likely alert and ready for action.
   • The iron gate leading to the city opened by itself.
   • The angel walked with Peter and then left him.

6. Peter could scarcely believe what was happening to him. He went to the meeting house to tell the believers he was free. He tried to keep their excitement quiet while he told the story. He was wise in that he didn't stay with those believers where possibly Herod's soldiers might have found him, but went somewhere else.

7. The church continued to trust God and meet together despite persecution (James was beheaded). They gathered together to pray – might have been praying all night. They earnestly prayed for Peter's release. They didn't believe God had answered!

8. You could focus on God's promises. Pray in your small group. Get a prayer partner. Share specific prayer requests – keep a record of them and thank God when they are answered.

Cover to Cover Every Day
Gain deeper knowledge of the Bible

Each issue of these bimonthly daily Bible-reading notes gives you insightful commentary on a book of the Old and New Testaments with reflections on a psalm each weekend by Philip Greenslade.

Enjoy contributions from two well-known authors every two months and over a five-year period you will be taken through the entire Bible.

 **Individual issues available in epub/Kindle formats**

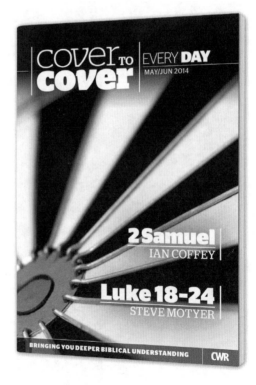

For current price or to order visit www.cwr.org.uk/subscriptions
Available online or from Christian bookshops.

Courses and seminars

Publishing and media

Conference facilities

Transforming lives

CWR's vision is to enable people to experience personal transformation through applying God's Word to their lives and relationships.

Our Bible-based training and resources help people around the world to:

- Grow in their walk with God
- Understand and apply Scripture to their lives
- Resource themselves and their church
- Develop pastoral care and counselling skills
- Train for leadership
- Strengthen relationships, marriage and family life and much more.

Our insightful writers provide daily Bible-reading notes and other resources for all ages, and our experienced course designers and presenters have gained an international reputation for excellence and effectiveness.

CWR's Training and Conference Centres in Surrey and East Sussex, England, provide excellent facilities in idyllic settings – ideal for both learning and spiritual refreshment.

CWR Applying God's Word
to everyday life and relationships

CWR, Waverley Abbey House,
Waverley Lane, Farnham,
Surrey GU9 8EP, UK

Telephone: **+44 (0)1252 784700**
Email: **info@cwr.org.uk**
Website: **www.cwr.org.uk**

Registered Charity No 294387
Company Registration No 1990308

Dramatic new resource

The Creed – Belief in action
by Phin Hall

What we believe shapes how we live, but what exactly do we believe as Christians? The Apostles' Creed exists to remind God's people about who He is and what He has done, and continues to do, for us.
72-page booklet, 210x148mm
ISBN: 978-1-78259-202-0

1 Peter – Good reasons for hope
by Dave Edwins

As Christians, what reason do we have to hope in a hostile world? How can we respond to unjust suffering? Peter's letter to his fellow Christians shows that then, as now, the answer lies in who we are in Christ.
72-page booklet, 210x148mm
ISBN: 978-1-78259-088-0

The bestselling *Cover to Cover* Bible Study Series

1 Corinthians
Growing a Spirit-filled church
ISBN: 978-1-85345-374-8

2 Corinthians
Restoring harmony
ISBN: 978-1-85345-551-3

1 Peter
Good reasons for hope
ISBN: 978-1-78259-088-0

1 Timothy
Healthy churches –
effective Christians
ISBN: 978-1-85345-291-8

23rd Psalm
The Lord is my shepherd
ISBN: 978-1-85345-449-3

2 Timothy and Titus
Vital Christianity
ISBN: 978-1-85345-338-0

Acts 1–12
Church on the move
ISBN: 978-1-85345-574-2

Acts 13–28
To the ends of the earth
ISBN: 978-1-85345-592-6

Barnabas
Son of encouragement
ISBN: 978-1-85345-911-5

Bible Genres
Hearing what the Bible really says
ISBN: 978-1-85345-987-0

Daniel
Living boldly for God
ISBN: 978-1-85345-986-3

Ecclesiastes
Hard questions and
spiritual answers
ISBN: 978-1-85345-371-7

Elijah
A man and his God
ISBN: 978-1-85345-575-9

Ephesians
Claiming your inheritance
ISBN: 978-1-85345-229-1

Esther
For such a time as this
ISBN: 978-1-85345-511-7

Fruit of the Spirit
Growing more like Jesus
ISBN: 978-1-85345-375-5

Galatians
Freedom in Christ
ISBN: 978-1-85345-648-0

Genesis 1–11
Foundations of reality
ISBN: 978-1-85345-404-2

God's Rescue Plan
Finding God's fingerprints
on human history
ISBN: 978-1-85345-294-9

Great Prayers of the Bible
Applying them to our lives today
ISBN: 978-1-85345-253-6

Hebrews
Jesus – simply the best
ISBN: 978-1-85345-337-3

Hosea
The love that never fails
ISBN: 978-1-85345-290-1

Isaiah 1–39
Prophet to the nations
ISBN: 978-1-85345-510-0

Isaiah 40–66
Prophet of restoration
ISBN: 978-1-85345-550-6

For current prices or to order visit www.cwr.org.uk/store
Available online or from Christian bookshops.

NATIONAL DISTRIBUTORS

UK: (and countries not listed below)
CWR, Waverley Abbey House, Waverley Lane, Farnham, Surrey GU9 8EP.
Tel: (01252) 784700 Outside UK (44) 1252 784700

AUSTRALIA: KI Entertainment, Unit 21 317-321 Woodpark Road, Smithfield, New South Wales 2164. Tel: 1 800 850 777 Fax: 02 9604 3699. Email: sales@kientertainment.com.au

CANADA: David C Cook Distribution Canada, PO Box 98, 55 Woodslee Avenue, Paris, Ontario N3L 3E5. Tel: 1800 263 2664 Email: joy.kearley@davidccook.ca

GHANA: Challenge Enterprises of Ghana, PO Box 5723, Accra.
Tel: (021) 222437/223249 Fax: (021) 226227 Email: ceg@africaonline.com.gh

HONG KONG: Cross Communications Ltd, 1/F, 562A Nathan Road, Kowloon.
Tel: 2780 1188 Fax: 2770 6229 Email: cross@crosshk.com

INDIA: Crystal Communications, Plot No. 125, Road No. 7, T.M.C, Mahendra Hills, East Marredpally, Secunderabad - 500026 Tel/Fax: (040) 27737145
Email: crystal_edwj@rediffmail.com

KENYA: Keswick Books and Gifts Ltd, PO Box 10242-00400, Nairobi.
Tel: (020) 2226047/312639 Email: sales.keswick@africaonline.co.ke

MALAYSIA: Canaanland Distributors Sdn Bhd, No. 25 Jalan PJU 1A/41B, NZX Commercial Centre, Ara Jaya, 47301 Petaling Jaya, Selangor. Tel: (03) 7885 0540/1/2 Fax: (03) 7885 0545 Email: info@canaanland.com.my

Salvation Publishing & Distribution Sdn Bhd, 23 Jalan SS 2/64, 47300 Petaling Jaya, Selangor. Tel: (03) 78766411/78766797 Fax: (03) 78757066/78756360
Email: info@salvationbookcentre.com

NEW ZEALAND: KI Entertainment, Unit 21 317-321 Woodpark Road, Smithfield, New South Wales 2164, Australia. Tel: 0 800 850 777 Fax: +612 9604 3699
Email: sales@kientertainment.com.au

NIGERIA: FBFM, Helen Baugh House, 96 St Finbarr's College Road, Akoka, Lagos.
Tel: (+234) 01-7747429, 08075201777, 08186337699, 08154453905
Email: fbfm_1@yahoo.com

PHILIPPINES: OMF Literature Inc, 776 Boni Avenue, Mandaluyong City.
Tel: (02) 531 2183 Fax: (02) 531 1960 Email: gloadlaon@omflit.com

SINGAPORE: Alby Commercial Enterprises Pte Ltd, 95 Kallang Avenue #04-00, AIS Industrial Building, 339420. Tel: (65) 629 27238 Fax: (65) 629 27235
Email: marketing@alby.com.sg

SOUTH AFRICA: Life Media & Distribution, Unit 20, Tungesten Industrial Park, 7 C R Swart Drive, Strydompark 2125 Tel: (+27) 0117924277 Fax: (+27) 0117924512 Email: orders@lifemedia.co.za

SRI LANKA: Christombu Publications (Pvt) Ltd, Bartleet House, 65 Braybrooke Place, Colombo 2. Tel: (+941) 2421073/2447665. Email: christombupublications@gmail.com

USA: David C Cook Distribution Canada, PO Box 98, 55 Woodslee Avenue, Paris, Ontario N3L 3E5, Canada. Tel: 1800 263 2664. Email: joy.kearley@davidccook.ca

For email addresses, visit the CWR website: www.cwr.org.uk
CWR is a Registered Charity - Number 294387
CWR is a Limited Company registered in England - Registration Number 1990308